There Is Purpose in Your Pain

By Angie Taylor Reames

Pure Thoughts Publishing, LLC

In life we deal with so much pain.

Though we dread experiencing pain- it is true that with pain comes growth and change. We learn something each time we experience pain. We have a choice- What we can do as a response to experienced pain is choose to use it for growth in a positive way or allow it to steal our sanity and rob us of any happiness that we have.

I am thankful that God looks over me and wakes me up- even in my painful situations. I am absolutely grateful that He allows me to understand and recognize that there is purpose in my pain. There is not a moment in my life where pain did not birth something, be it spiritual, physical, mental, emotionally- I know that there is a purpose for the pain that I endure.

Prayerfully, I ask that you find a way to grasp the pain and get the lesson from what it is that God is trying to teach you. It is with genuine humbleness that I write this book. This book is for those of you who are dealing with life and the situations that are presented to you as it concerns your growth. I pray that you are able to grow from your pain and realize you have a purpose. We are not mistakes. We are not could haves, we are not victims. We are victorious and we are undefeated. You are worthy and you have purpose.

From the Author

I dedicate this book to the individuals who deal with pain; whether it's secretly or publicly. I pray that you are blessed in knowing that there is purpose in your pain. God has a purpose for your life. Romans 8:29 says it best- "And we know that all things work together for good to them that Love God, to them who are the called according to his purpose". There is definitely purpose in your pain and you must tap into what God has blessed you with. God will never give you anything that you can't handle- all that you are going through, have gone through, or will go through helps you find your purpose. There is purpose in your pain.

In this book, I touch on points of pain- I highlight different types of hurt but I also want you, the reader to understand that having a relationship with God, even when I did not understand was what saved me.

It was what healed me. God gets the glory out of the most painful situations of our lives as well.

Also from the Author:

Perfect Imperfection: I am who I am

A book of Inspirational Poetry

Published: August 2015

Available on www.angiereames.com and www.amazon.com

Booking information for speaking engagements:

Website: www.angiereames.com

Email: angie.reames@yahoo.com

Phone: 803-229-0936

Table of Contents

Pain and Response

You may notice that I refer to myself a lot in this book. I am not being selfish. However, I know how to tell my story because it is MY story. No one can tell your story or your testimony like you. So please allow me to share my pain, my life, my misery in hopes that you will be blessed from what I have victoriously achieved. I am not boasting about what God has brought me through- But I am grateful that He will use me and my imperfections to bless others.

It is said that you minister through your misery. It is with esteemed gratefulness that I am allowed to say "YES" to what God has assigned me to do.

The inside cover picture in this book speaks volumes. In December 2015, I had the opportunity of visiting a "historical place". The memories that were in this place opened up so many emotions that I had no idea were there. When I was a child, because of their reasons- my parents separated. My mother took my siblings and me and we moved to another county. As a child, I was taken away from my known routine of doing things and I adapted to the new norm. I don't blame anyone for the separations. Although as a child, I did not understand what was going on, as an adult I have learned that everyone has their own journeys and that was a part of theirs-which in turn what started my very own journey.

The historical place that I visited was that house we moved to after the separation. I remember parking at the front of the house In December 2015 and it looked so much different, with my adult eyes-those same eyes that belonged to me as a child. But the adult eyes that have seen so much, that have cried tears of pain, the eyes that have forgiven others without an apology. As a child, I saw this safe house that was filled with love and family (my mom, sister, and brother). I went back to visit that place- for the first time in close to thirty years.

There were so many things that were in my mind. My emotions began to run wild- I began reflecting on my past. The pain that I unknowingly harbored in after the separation somehow manifested. I later realized that the separation was the beginning of MY journey- or what some may call LIFE. My life and all memories began when I was about five or six years old. My life begun when my mother and father had their differences, developing me to be the woman I am to be. I have learned so much from their struggles and I am grateful for the strength that their life gave me.

I have found myself in deep thought wondering if my parents actually realize that there was a purpose in what occurred in their life- That their purpose birthed so much in me and my ministry, my purpose. The negative mindset, pain, and anger on some days, although it was not an overnight process- turned into something positive (or at least it is what I believe). I truly believe the words of Jeremiah 1:5(CEB)- "Before I created you in the womb, I knew you..."; and let me also mention Jeremiah 29:11(CEB), "I know the plans

I have in mind for you, declares the Lord; they are plans for peace, not disaster, to give you a future filled with hope." You can call me crazy if you want- but I TRUST GOD AND HIS PLANS FOR ME! I trust that my life is all according to His plans... This is where I begin doing my happy dance! I get excited about the Lord!!!

The beautiful thing about pain is there is purpose in it. There is purpose in the "going through" process.

I am not saying that we will agree with everything; however I firmly believe that the Lord will turn all bad things around so that they will work out for our good. See I could have dwelled over all the bad things that happened in life- but instead I focused on the good. What is the purpose of jumping in the negative pool and then drowning? What is the PURPOSE of skinny dipping in the NEGATIVITY pool- to be weighed down with depression, aggravation, disgust, anger, etc. - and left unable to stay afloat? WHAT is the purpose of diving into the Negative Pool when you refuse to trust the **lifeguard** to save you- because you have been trying to take matters into your own hand, you have not been trusting GOD(the lifeguard). You have been reaching your hands out trying to be saved by the world, and that isn't going to help. You have been attempting to be freed by the world. I have been there- Oh boy have I been there.

So, with all the weight that negativity puts on you to weigh you down, stress you out and cause you pain- it is best to just rid yourself of it. Understand, you get one life and it is better to give this life your best shot. Don't just exist. You deserve to be great! Don't voluntarily stay in a bad place, don't you voluntarily jump, dive and skinny dip in the negative pool. However, if you find yourself there- Pray that you are strengthened and you understand the purpose in your pain. You are too strong to be weak. That same energy that you are using to stay in the dark area of your life can be reversed so that you can be victorious- you do know that don't you?

Do not get complacent and comfortable in a bad situation- because you think that life has handed you a bad hand. Pick yourself up. If we continue to dwell on the bad things in life- how far will we get? Do you love yourself? Honestly, answer that question. If you understand what love is and you genuinely love yourself, you will invest time in yourself and not your pain and bad situation.

I think when we know better- we should do better- I believe that. So, I learned to do better when going through the situations. Yes, we all have stories and testimonies- and our stories will help others. I thank God, for allowing me to share my struggles to help others. Our struggles don't just occur just for us to go through- we go through things so that we can

help others. There is definitely ministry in our misery-
we are more than conquerors. I believe that I am a
CHAMP- you are too!

I am not ashamed of the things that I have
survived. I am not ashamed of what I have been
saved from. I am NOT ashamed. I have been
abandoned. I have been disrespected. I have been
abused. I have sinned. I am not perfect. I mess up. I
have been neglected. I have been judged. I have been
heartbroken. I have suffered- BUT I survived and I am
still here- Now that my friend is what you call
PURPOSE! What have you been through and
SURVIVED? Yes, you have purpose.

So, I have been through test and trials. I am here.
You have been through tests and trials. You are here.
Ok, so yes I am human and I don't always get it right.

I am not a superhero. I do not possess super powers.
There were so many times I wanted to give up.
Quitting used to be second nature for me. I would
take matters into my own hands and wherever the
chips landed was absolutely fine with me. (Thank God

for Grace and Mercy). When situations were out of my control, I used to get angry. There were times when I thought of taking the coward's way out and commit suicide, but I would have been selfish in doing so. Time after time I would beat myself up for not being in a better situation then I was in. I would torture myself for settling, wanting to blame others for my failures. Constantly, making excuses for everything that seemed hard to accomplish. I feared achievement. Who does that? The answer is someone who harbored pain and used it for an excuse not to do better. WOW! Yes pain can and will hinder you.

Looking back, I realize that pain has actually helped me in life. It really depends on how you want to look at it. No, I didn't always believe that it was helping me. Being numb to any emotions or feelings was my way of happiness. I felt that if I ignored the pain and swept it under the rug that it would disappear. Being naïve, I didn't realize that the pain was just accumulating and not being resolved. I found myself with a village of pain- which turned into anger and depression. Not realizing it at the time, but it helped me. Eventually, I had to deal with it. It made me strong; it made me aware of what I would actually accept and not allow. Facing the pain, helped me to realize that I am/was worth saving- that greater is in me!

Understand that pain can take you out- BUT it depends on your response. Pain does not own me. Pain does not own you. Be encouraged and know that with anything your response is important. My historical visit made me aware of the greatness that was planted in me as a young child. Have you revisited that place where your pain resides? FACE IT AND RESPOND. I chose to respond to that pain, when I knew better in a beneficial way. How will you respond to the pain of life? It is not okay to bury yourself while you are still alive. It is not okay to die while you are alive (Get it?). I am a CHAMP and you are too... So hello pain... you have been defeated. Game over!

What are some personal ways that you have dealt with pain and response?

_____

_____

_____

_____

_____

_____

_____

_____

_____

_____

_____

_____

_____

_____

_____

There Is Purpose In Your Pain

_____

_____

_____

_____

_____

_____

_____

_____

_____

_____

_____

_____

_____

_____

_____

_____

He will wipe away every tear from their eyes, and death shall be no more, neither shall there be mourning, nor crying, nor pain anymore, for the former things have passed away. Revelation 21:4

Angie Taylor Reames

Champ- Fighting Pain

Have you ever been in a situation where you attempted to run from pain? You find yourself pinned in a corner, what we so often call a rock and a hard place. Constantly being hit left and right, visions of your past flashing before your eyes, unaware of what the final verdict will be. When you feel that you have enough guts to run, you attempt to run from the pain. Then you realize that no matter where you go- you're STILL going to be right there. You run from the pain, the person, the place, the thing that hurt you only to realize that it is still right there with you. Trying to cover up all the pain, the fear, the pressure of the day, the headache, the sickness, the misunderstandings, the confusion... running from it-

12

and then realizing that it yet remains. So what is there to do? I am glad you asked...

I have dealt with different types of pain. I am sure you have to. But one thing that we have in common is that 'We did not give up'. There are times that I wanted to quit but I remained strong. Some of those times I felt like I was weak, not realizing God were strengthening me with each situation. I did not know at that moment what was going on or that my purpose was being manifested through all that I was enduring.

I have fought with so many things. I felt like I had lost. It's not that I lost the battles though, but I was being trained to be greater. I have gone through different support systems- different "friends"- and through it all God never left me. I have been knocked around and beat down- BUT I got back up! You got back up too! Some of the things that I was fighting with was only preparing me for greater.

Although, the pain is REAL and there are some things that we just don't want to believe. There are things that are revealed in the process. The process of growth and the process of purpose can be heavy. However, I truly believe that God never gives us anything that we can't handle. He has equipped us to be strong, great, successful, victorious… and He knows just what to give us.

So, with the battles of life I fought my hardest. I wanted to walk away from many opponents and challenges. I have cried, thrown things, screamed- I guess some would call it throwing a tantrum. Regardless of what it is called- I knew no other way of releasing my frustrations without feeling like I had failed. I was not giving up- however I was trying to maintain my sanity.

Staying in the boxing ring of life requires much focus. I have had to remind myself that I can do it. Focusing is not always the easiest thing. There are moments, when distractions come into play. Those are the moments when you have to come to grips with what really matters. A distraction is just that THING that attempts to get your attention from what

REALLY matters. A distraction will put you on a journey for a long route when what you should have been focusing on is right around the corner. I have had to maintain my focus, but disregarding the distractions was really a challenge.

Fighting the pain that goes everywhere I go. Attempting to go toe to toe with that seizure, that morning migraine, that brokenness, and that heartache can be really hard. Though releasing the frustrations in my own little way seemed to be so convenient- it never removed what the real issue is. In other words, you cannot run from that which is attached to you. The pain was attached to me. The depression was attached to me. I learned to fight though. It was either defeat that pain or allow it to consume me.

Be careful with what you allow to attach to you. Spirits are transferrable. There are some people in our lives that will make us feel like we are losers because that is the mentality that they are accustomed to. We refer to the people we are close to as our circle, but are you allowing unnecessary people in your circle? I understand that we are in contact with people for reasons, seasons, and even lifetimes. Be careful that you are not babysitting seasonal friends. Those types of relationships will definitely have you feeling like you are losing. Certain attachments will have you covering up the real you because you are being fake just to maintain a relationship with others and it is not worth it.

Okay, what must I do in order to win? Trust a God who never loses. Yes that is it! There are many battles that I attempted to take into my own hands. Well, actually there are many battles that I did take into my own hands. This is one of the many situations when I realized that I was nothing without HIM. I know that I am unable to function without the Lord. The Lord makes me whole! The Lord fights my battles and He guides me to be strong. He guides me to be a winner and He guides me to be A CHAMP!

Of all the things that I have fought, Pain has been one that hurts in an indescribable way. The fact that fighting pain was something that I was not able to run from, it felt like DEAD weight. I felt depressed, frustrated, and weary. The process hurt so badly. I was not sure if I was coming or going on some days. I tried running from pain and I always found myself in the most peaceful place. See there is purpose in the pain- I found myself growing. Though the fighting seemed so right- it was wrong. Only thing my fighting was doing was making me feel weak. I was completely insane for thinking I could win without God. Eventually, I would find myself back at the beginning of where I started. Until I submitted to what God was telling me to do.

There are times when we feel like we are drowning in our own sorrow. We may feel hopeless. But I say to you-

Never Give Up!

Trust God!

Listen to What God is saying to you!

Let God Fight for You (Be equipped with whole armor of God)

Remember, God loves you no matter what pain you are going through- He wants you to call on Him so that you can tell everyone how good He has been to you. You are A Champ but remember all the Glory belongs to God!

There Is Purpose In Your Pain

What are some personal ways that you have dealt with fighting pain?

_____

_____

_____

_____

_____

_____

_____

_____

_____

_____

_____

_____

_____

_____

_____

_____

_____

_____

_____

_____

_____

_____

_____

_____

_____

_____

_____

_____

_____

_____

_____

The Lord is my rock and my fortress and my deliverer, my God, my rock, in whom I take refuge, my shield, and the horn of my salvation, my stronghold. Psalm 18:2

Mourning- Death Pain

was numb. I was empty. I got sick. I cried. I screamed. I missed my Papa. There are times when we take life for granted. We assume that the people we love are always going to be around. Then when we lose them- it is too late. Apart of me seemed to leave when he left. My granddad was special to me. I never realized how much he meant to me until I got older and I started seeing the qualities in him that I wanted to always have in my life. My granddaddy was a hardworking man. He was an imperfect man, who made no excuses for it. He was always there for me when I needed him. He knew how to love even if it was misunderstood.

Angie Taylor Reames

My granddaddy, Mr. William "Sonny Boy" Magazine was a man of few words but when he needed to speak he did. I remember when we would have conversations and I would be talking- his response was normally a nod and a grunt. I can smile because I know our hearts were connected, with love and joy. I feel that he understood me. I can actually say that he was the one man that would tell me to keep up the good work. He would say things like,

"hmph you doing good". He was an 'old school tree shade' mechanic (the best), I got a newer car and of course I had to take it to let him see it. Smiling, he said to me that the motor was a lot different then what he was used to. I truly miss him. There is so much more that I could say- however I just wanted share briefly my mourning.

There are times in our lives when we hold onto that death pain. We assume that it is better to hold it in verses expressing ourselves, because we seem to always be misunderstood. Well, when we hold in pain it usually released through anger, hatred and

22

bitterness. It is never easy to say goodbye to a loved one forever. We get accustomed to seeing them, relying on them when we need things, being there, hugging them, hearing their laughter or perhaps wiping their tears. So, when it is time to say goodbye we somehow, at times not knowing become selfish. There are times that our loved ones have suffered and are better off not being in that pain anymore. We have lost loved ones in tragic accidents, sickness, suicides, murders, but GOD knows what you can handle (Trust me, you are still here- you were destined to be great). There are times when they have fulfilled their purpose on earth. We as humans somehow forget about the time that we have shared with those that we love and care about.

Just as we are born, we will die. That same logic is so with our loved ones as well. We have to learn to love on purpose, with purpose and let the death pain manifest more purpose. There is purpose in the pain! We just have to come to the realization that we deserve to live in peace and know that our loved ones will rest in peace. Our life goes on; you cannot operate in your full purpose by allowing yourself to dwell amongst the dead. It is not easy, but if you operate in your calling, giving the glory to God- it will definitely be worth it.

God has a purpose for everything we go through, Instead of mourning constantly, I channeled that energy in doing something that my Papa would be proud of- He was always proud of me for being a great mother to my children and doing great in my life. I will never let him down, I refuse to dwell in dead places but I will invest greatness in my life as if he was still alive.

I advise you to learn to invest in YOU. Free yourself from that death pain and remember that there is purpose in your pain. Never underestimate the power of prayer and believe that God will never fail you. You have a purpose. What legacy will you leave?

There Is Purpose In Your Pain

What are some personal ways that you have dealt with mourning?

_____

_____

_____

_____

_____

_____

_____

_____

_____

_____

_____

_____

_____

_____

_____

_____

_____

_____

_____

_____

_____

_____

_____

_____

_____

_____

_____

_____

_____

_____

_____

_____

_____

The Lord is near to the brokenhearted and saves the crushed in spirit. Psalm 34:18

Broken Heart- Pain and Relationships

Oh the agony and heartache that we feel when we are heartbroken. We feel like everything we have invested in a person is now gone. In relationships, we get accustomed to expecting so much that when it doesn't go the way we want, we become extremely disappointed. We allow ourselves to get depressed, cry ourselves to sleep, get stressed, get sick, and the like. Our pain makes us want to hurt other people. When we experience a broken heart, we sometimes get belligerent and react out of character. Heartache (heartbreak) can lead us down a dark path of anger and sadness.

When experiencing a broken heart- we should not lose who we are. Our life is not over. Some people start other habits to cover up the pain. There are some people that start doing drugs, they start drinking, they think less of themselves- they begin sleeping with numerous sexual partners. The pain sends them into an identity crisis. Pain is pain but some pain hurts more than others.

Many of us hurt more from a broken heart because we have invested time into an individual trying to make them be who we want them to be. We get disappointed and heartbroken because their flaws are not accepted by us. Many of us deal with hurt and pain in relationships because we are trying to fill a void- from something that we may not have had in our lives. When you attempt to fill a void with the wrong filler- it is rejected. Thing is the rejection was never planned.

There are some people that set themselves up for failure and aren't equipped to handle rejections. Some people have been dealing with rejections all of their lives and are still unaware of how to handle it. Instead of facing the rejection they run from it. They find that they have been running all of their lives. They have been running all of their lives from something and never know how to handle it. Even as adults they invest time into negativity and remain unaware that lots of the heartache is self-infliction. You will never fully operate in being your best self and full potential, if you never deal with who you are.

Your broken heart is a reflection of how well you love yourself. OUCH! When you know your worth, it won't be so easy to allow people to hurt you to the extent that you lose who you are. I never said it won't hurt but you have control over what you allow yourself to do. When you know your worth, you will be able to function in your full potential and at your known value. Also, learn to know the person you are and are growing to be- because everything is not always everybody else's fault. Taking responsibility for your actions will help you become a better person in the midst of all the pain that you are feeling.

There are many times that people refuse to forgive those that hurt them. Why should you forgive? I am so glad that you ask. You forgive so that you can move on. You forgive so that you won't have all that pain harboring inside. You forgive so that you can be free from bondage.

You should never love anyone more than you love the Lord. Many times people will idolize that man/woman- they will confide in him/her before seeking the Lord. The Lord is a jealous God- so do not be surprised when your sin love does not work out the way you expected it to. God wants the glory in everything. Build your relationship with HIM and HE will direct your paths and send you the person who will help you become a better person.

Your broken heart, your rejections, your pain, and your misunderstandings, are all equipping you to be stronger and to walk in your purpose. You are valuable and you have a purpose! It is important to know WHOSE you are.

There Is Purpose In Your Pain

What are some personal ways that you have dealt with heartbreak?

_____

_____

_____

_____

_____

_____

_____

_____

_____

_____

_____

_____

_____

_____

_____

_____

_____

_____

_____

_____

_____

_____

_____

_____

_____

_____

_____

_____

_____

_____

_____

_____

For I consider that the sufferings of this present time are not worth comparing with the glory that is to be revealed to us. Romans 8:18

Truth- Pain and Marriage

Well where do I start? As a female- most of us look forward to our wedding day even as we are growing up. We look forward to wearing our exquisite and elegant gowns. We anticipate being surrounded by family, our dad (or loved one) giving us away at the altar, planning our reception, and being optimistic on designing our wedding cake. Yes, most of us do this! We get so caught up in the colors and the fit of the dress. We all want some type of uniqueness on our special day even if that means having a small celebration. Though the most important thing in planning the wedding is usually not thought of, we still continue. That most important thing is the planning of the MARRIAGE.

Angie Taylor Reames

We normally never know what we want in a spouse as we have the beautiful vision of our dream wedding running through our minds. Usually, we just know what we DON'T want. We know we don't want a broke man, an ugly man, an annoying man, etc. Please know that this is not being written to put anyone down, however it is to discuss the pain in the marriage-The marriage that we never planned. We get so caught up in the small details of our big day that we don't think of planning how we will spend the rest of our lives. Some plan the wedding and not think of the marriage.

Marriage requires work! Not just from one person but from both parties. Many times people enter into marriages with the idea that they will live happily ever after. Well there is WORK that is required to live happily ever after. Again, there will be expectancies and honestly there will be disappointments. There will be pain, trials, tribulations, tears, and everyday really is not going to be GREAT. That doesn't mean you give up- that doesn't mean you quit at the first sign of him/her not covering their mouth when they sneeze. That doesn't mean that you flee because they left the toilet seat up. Are the issues that are making you want to leave based off of what you are dealing with personally? Is your life in danger? Are you being selfish?

There are many times when individuals bring all of their personal issues in the relationship when in actuality a marriage is the coming of two people becoming ONE! So, if you are dealing with something discuss it with your spouse. Communication is very important. The lack of communication can be very painful. I do believe that words hurt but you must invest in your marriage exactly what you want it to be. Therefore having an open line of communication helps to know what the other person is thinking or feeling.

Let me say this though; stop thinking that you are perfect in all of your decisions because you are not the only one to live on those decisions. It's not always about you!!! You are not the only person in the marriage. Some tend to think that it's all about them.

But what if the shoe was on the other foot and you were made to feel that you didn't matter or your feelings were not important? That would hurt and though there is purpose in your pain, no one deserves to be made to feel that they aren't important- No matter who you are. The bible says, and two shall become one. So take into consideration that you are not alone in the marriage.

Another thing, you will experience much pain if you allow OTHER people inside of what is supposed to be you and your spouses' relationship. See the truth is that there will be people that do not want to see you happy. They will probably show up at your wedding, buy you a gift, smile in your face, take pictures with you for social media posting, and HATE you with jealousy. Be careful of the people you allow in your personal space, in your marriage space- no one else is supposed to be there except God.

So pain, it comes when one (sometimes both) person(s) feels unappreciated. It comes when there is a lack of love. Pain occurs when two people stop trying to love each other more daily. It comes from lack of trust. Pain happens in marriages too.

There are people looking at how you handle your marriage. There are people who look up to you, they want what you have. But those that look for you and admire your happiness and joyous marriage fail to recognize that work that you put in. You must sow into your marriage that which you plan to harvest. If you are thankful for your spouse then you need to thank God daily for him or her. We all make mistakes, forgiveness is very important in your marriage. To be in a marriage with a person and not harboring feelings of non-forgiveness is extremely unhealthy for the marriage.

Communication and forgiveness are two key factors in marriage. You also have to know how to cater to your spouse. One must know how to be supportive, respectful, understanding, humble, loving, passionate, kind, and responsible to name a few. But one must also know that God is first in the marriage. If you understand that your spouse has a calling on their life then it is important to respect that. Respect that you have a spouse who loves the Lord. It is great to pray together and grow spiritually. When your marriage can grow through pain, it builds your purpose. God wants the glory out of everything that we do, learn to give Him the glory from your marriage as well.

Yes, there is pain in marriage. But always remember what is important. Do not focus on the pain by burying yourself in the pit of bitterness and melancholy. There is something purposeful about coming out of that dark place. You are destined for greatness. Your marriage depends on you. So, even if your purpose is to help someone else get through a drought in their marriage, create a blog, hug someone when you notice the pain, well at least you would be aware that your pain is not in vain.

Remember that no one is perfect and we all got through something in our lives. There are some people who believe that they are perfect individuals in a marriage and they do no wrong. Well you have to reevaluate yourself because if you believe that you have no fault then you are guilty of the blame game-that is a problem in itself. It is okay to do a self-evaluation and adjust accordingly. Not only will it benefit you, it will benefit your marriage. You are not perfect, we all make mistakes and we must be willing to be held accountable for our actions. Your marriage depends on you. What God has joined, let no man separate.

Angie Taylor Reames

What are some personal ways that you have dealt with pain in your marriage?

_____

_____

_____

_____

_____

_____

_____

_____

_____

_____

_____

_____

_____

_____

_____

_____

There Is Purpose In Your Pain

_____
_____
_____
_____
_____
_____
_____
_____
_____
_____
_____
_____
_____
_____
_____
_____
_____
_____

At least I can take comfort in this: Despite the pain, I have not denied the words of the Holy One. Job 6:10

Prayer and Pain in the Present

So you may not believe this but this chapter was not included in the pre planning of the book. I found myself in this type of pain as I was typing the last chapter and out of obedience to God I began typing. This chapter came from my present situation. I am currently, at this very moment on June 11, 2016 sitting in an ICU room typing and of course watching my daddy sleep. I never imagined being in this place, not with my daddy or anyone. I never knew that I would be feeling the emotions of pain in my present situation.

I think I mentioned in the beginning of this book, definitely in "Perfect Imperfection-I am who I am" that I am my mama's baby but I am my daddy's ONLY child. Yes, I am a daddy's girl. He and I stick together because of that man I can say that I am "Taylor Made".

My dad got sick and although he has siblings, he has no spouse- As he and I always say, "We're all that we got". I have been beside him (not bragging or complaining) all throughout this process and I am not going anywhere. This is the first time he and I experienced this as it relates to his health. Of course throughout life we both experienced different situations and we were there for one another. But this time it was different. He is helpless and I am alone.

I found myself looking around for someone during the surgery and I was alone. My phone was getting messages and calls but for about six hours straight, no one was there. I read books, I read the bible, I got on my phone, and I did everything! The one thing that I found that helped was PRAYER. Though I was alone dealing with the pain of not knowing what my dad was going through on the surgical table, knowing I could not physically be there. I knew that prayer was one way of helping him. When I looked around and no one was there except strangers in the waiting area dealing with their own personal issues- I began to grow weary.

While battling the Only Child Syndrome, because I could not call on a sibling to share my emotions with- I found myself getting emotional. My dad had been hospitalized, now in surgery, going through all of this and I felt horrible for him. Although, I trust God and I know that His plans are for us to prosper, I felt abandoned. Here I am going through the issues of my own life and now having to make sure my "Baby" as I call him, was ok.

I realized although I had to keep everyone updated because they were "worrying", kept myself together, be there for my family, and make sure I remained strong for my daddy- I still had to trust God. I knew that although there were people who I could not see or touch, yet I knew that they were praying for him. I knew that they were coming, I knew I had support, I knew that there were people who loved us. I realize that in the moments when I felt alone- that God was orchestrating HIS healing powers, His strength and angels were covering us.

Even in this very moment while I sit alone. I know that there are people who are going through something worst. I know that I am blessed beyond measure to know that I am able to count on people for prayer although no one was present. See there is something powerful in knowing that even when it seems that no one is present or physically there-don't get discouraged- it doesn't mean that they are not praying. There is something prevailing in knowing the difference between prayer and presence.

My present pain is not my final process- there is purpose here and I will push to get to my destiny in Christ Jesus. You should too.

What are some personal ways that you are currently experiencing pain and do you see its purpose?

_____

_____

_____

_____

_____

_____

_____

_____

_____

_____

_____

_____

_____

_____

_____

There Is Purpose In Your Pain

_____
_____
_____
_____
_____
_____
_____
_____
_____
_____
_____
_____
_____
_____
_____
_____
_____
_____

For I know the plans I have for you, declares the Lord, Plans to prosper you and not to harm you, plans to give you hope and a future. Jeremiah 29:11

Forgiveness

Forgiveness is freedom. There are so many of us that assumed we would benefit from holding onto something or holding a grudge against that person or those people that have caused us pain. We have gone to extremes to make sure we don't look in that persons direction when they are in our presence, we will even cross the street to avoid them, we will take the long ride home to keep from passing their house, or change our entire lifestyle just so we won't or wouldn't have to forgive him, her or them. But what about you?

The lack of forgiving causes more pain. There are so many people that feel that if they do not forgive a person that they have control over that individual or those individuals. But that is the complete opposite. So, let's just say that you had a friend, (let's call this friend "Willie") that betrayed you. Willie got on social media and told everyone your secret- you know that one that you only told Willie. That secret that you were embarrassed about but you needed to vent one day and you told Willie in confidence. Well now Willie is upset with you for whatever petty reason they can think of. So here it is the post on social media with all of your embarrassing business, broadcasted for everyone to see, like, comment, and share! Now you are furious, you can think of 100 things you want to do to Willie, but instead you decide to hate instead.

Now you are walking around with all this hatred and bitterness in your heart, in your mind, and it has contaminated your spirit. Your blood pressure is rising. You have taken on an entire new person. Not only are you having to put out energy to focus on being your normal self-but now you are also investing in the energy of being negative and hateful just so you do not have to forgive someone.

Forgive! So many people say it is hard to forgive. Well it is just as hard not to forgive. You are causing more pain by allowing that hatred to contaminate your life. The person or those people that you are mad with and choosing not to forgive have now become a part of your daily living. You have become so accustomed to avoiding them until you have lost yourself hiding behind the pain and bitterness. The people have invaded your sanity.

You are now so into making sure Uncle John(who molested you) knows that you hate him, Cousin Shawn(who raped you), Willie(who betrayed you), daddy (who didn't protect you), mommy(who left you)- you are harboring all of this hatred for the sake of not forgiving. What is it benefiting you? The fact that you choose not to forgive is hindering your growth. How? Well simple, you are still mentally in that same place THAT thing took place.

Spiritual- How many times have you messed up and God forgave you?

There Is Purpose In Your Pain

When you choose not to forgive you allow others to control your mindset, the way you think, and the way you process things. Believe it or not, you are now adjusting your life to cater around them, whether to hurt them or hold them hostage. Sad truth is you are the hurt one and the one in bondage. You have to forgive- it frees you. Also, it is perfectly okay to let the other person know that you forgive them.

So many times we walk around with the weight of the world on our shoulders. There are times when we must be the bigger person, at times for ourselves. We deserve to be free. Luke 4:18 says "The Spirit of the

Lord is on me, because he has anointed me to proclaim freedom for the prisoners and recovery of sight for the blind, TO SET THE OPPRESSED FREE."

You can be free from hatred, bitterness, oppression, and depression. Will you allow yourself to forgive?

I pray that you do not go to your death bed with ill feelings toward someone else. Forgive them. Stop allowing others to be the gas that makes your engine run. Stop creating pain for yourself. Use the hurt that they have caused so that you can help others. There is purpose in your pain. Your destiny is not in your last destination. You have been treating yourself like the victim. You are the survivor. I challenge you to forgive those that hurt you. Your life depends on it.

Once you have forgiven those that hurt you- make sure you forgive yourself! Do not blame yourself. We declare victory, no blame games! You're a survivor!

It may not be an easy task however, the task is worth it.

What are some personal ways that you have had to deal with forgiving someone?

_____

_____

_____

_____

_____

_____

_____

_____

_____

_____

_____

_____

_____

_____

_____

Angie Taylor Reames

_____

_____
_____
_____
_____
_____
_____
_____
_____
_____
_____
_____
_____
_____
_____

Matthew 6:14-15 - For if you forgive other people when they sin against you, your heavenly Father will also forgive you. But if you do not forgive others their sins, your Father will not forgive your sins.

Suicide

Suicide (Self Murder) is when one intentionally causing their own death. Mental illness usually causes one to commit suicide. Depression, bipolar disorder, alcoholism, drug abuse, schizophrenia, personality disorders, bullying, stress, financial issues, and even relationship problems are all factors that may result in suicide.

Suicide is no solution to any problem. If you are having suicidal thoughts, seek help. Seek guidance. Do not be embarrassed. Suicidal thoughts are more common than we think. Suicide is the 10th leading cause of death in the US for all ages. Suicide is real however, there are ways to eliminate this tragic form of death. Seek medical help, get psychological help, contact a therapist, talk to your pastor, talk to someone you trust, and learn to love yourself- flaws and all.

The enemy wants you to believe that you are not worthy! The enemy wants you to lose your mind. Your purpose is far greater than anything that the enemy can throw your direction. When the enemy feels like you aren't able to be destroyed, the mission of the enemy will be to distract you.

You have a purpose, if that were not true- the enemy wouldn't be working so hard to take you out.

When you feel that you are not worth it, loved, needed, or like you do not matter. Start calling on the name of Jesus. Call Him, and He will save you. You are too valuable and you matter.

Not many people like to discuss this topic. Just know that you are not alone and that there is help. See it. Love who God has created you to be, embrace yourself, and know that you matter. You will not live life feeling like you are in hell and then die and go there! God loves you too much. God is Faithful!

There Is Purpose In Your Pain

The National Suicide Prevention Lifeline number is 1-800-273-8255 and help is available 24 hours a day.

What are some personal ways that you have dealt with suicide and suicidal thoughts?

_____

_____

_____

_____

_____

_____

_____

_____

_____

_____

_____

_____

_____

_____

_____

_____

_____

_____

_____

_____

_____

_____

_____

_____

_____

_____

_____

_____

_____

_____

_____

_____

Do you not know that you are God's temple and that God's Spirit dwells in you? If anyone destroys

God's temple, God will destroy him. For God's temple is holy, and you are that temple. I Corinthians 3:16&17

Be not overly wicked, neither be a fool. Why should you die before your time? Ecclesiastes 7:17

Addiction and Abuse

Addiction is the fact or condition of being addicted to a particular substance, person, thing, or activity. Addiction could be a medical condition, a spiritual condition, or a personal created condition. Addiction is when we choose to depend on something, be obsessed with, be infatuated with, or be enslaved to something.

So many times we get handicapped by an addiction. We procrastinate on seeking help. We allow our flesh to convince us that we have to be dependent on the drugs, on the alcohol, on the bad relationship, etc. We think that our strength comes from that infatuation- temporary release cannot compare to permanent freedom. Do not lose yourself in that thing that you have allowed yourself to be addicted to.

Over 100 people die daily from drug overdose.

Over 20 Million Americans, 12 years and over have an addiction- not including tobacco

Over 2 million people with addictions depend on both alcohol and illegal drugs

Your life is too important. Get your life back. The alcohol does not control you and nor does the drugs. Again, I remind you that there is purpose in your pain.

Abuse is the improper use of something, to be treated with cruelty, violence, misused, and/or mistreatment. Abuse can be physical, sexual, financial, digital, emotional and or verbal. Understand you are not alone. So many people have experienced abuse. There is no excuse for abuse and no one deserves to be abused. Not even you.

There is assistance. You are not a victim. If you are reading this then you are a survivor. Seek help. You deserve more than being abused.

Angie Taylor Reames

For help call 1-800-799-7233 or visit www.thehotline.org.

There Is Purpose In Your Pain

What are some personal ways that you have dealt with addiction and abuse?

_____

_____

_____

_____

_____

_____

_____

_____

_____

_____

_____

_____

_____

_____

_____

_____

_____

Angie Taylor Reames

_____
_____
_____
_____
_____
_____
_____
_____
_____
_____
_____
_____
_____
_____

No temptation has overtaken you except what is common to mankind. And God is faithful; he will not let you be tempted beyond what you can bear. But

There Is Purpose In Your Pain

when you are tempted, he will also provide a way out
so you can endure it. I Corinthians 10:13

Where is God in all of this?

Often we wonder where God is when we are experiencing pain and discomfort. We tend to question "Why me God?"? We seem to lose focus and we often lose faith. Our lives seem to have taken the wrong exit on the highways of life and we at times find ourselves at a dead end. We are left wondering, where is God?

Well I want to share some clarity on this- from experience. I have three points I want to share concerning this:

1. God never left- There are times that we need to reconnect to HIM. We get so distracted with all the wrong, giving it our time and

energy, failing to acknowledge or call on the Lord. We get so consumed in all of the issues, distractions, and dead ends that we lose our faith. We begin investing time into what it is that we should be trusting God to deliver us from. God never left, WE DID! Get connected with God, trust Him, and keep your faith.

2. Why not you- we are so quick to wonder why we are going through things. We get sick, WHY ME? We get depressed, WHY ME? We experience death, WHY ME? Well why not you? God has given you the armor to endure and you can do all things through Him who gives you strength. He knows exactly what we can handle. We cannot afford to get comfortable in a place and when pain comes we feel that our entire life is over. Well please understand when you get too comfortable, nothing grows. You are being shaken to be pressed to your purpose. God loves us and He

only wants what is best for us. So, next time you ask "WHY me", make sure you answer WHY NOT ME...

3. Stop giving the devil credit- We are so quick to blame the devil. Well just know that there are times when we are being pulled on so that God will get the GLORY out of our lives. Everything is not always the devil. Stop giving the devil credit when God is simply trying to make us greater. To God Be the Glory!

There Is Purpose In Your Pain

What are some moments when you thought that God left you?

_____

_____

_____

_____

_____

_____

_____

_____

_____

_____

_____

_____

_____

_____

_____

_____

_____

Angie Taylor Reames

_____

_____

_____

_____

_____

_____

_____

_____

_____

_____

_____

_____

_____

_____

_____

I tell you, whoever publicly acknowledges me before others, the Son of Man will also acknowledge before the angels of God. Luke 12:8

Workbook Insert

B elow are lists of questions that can be reviewed and studied. The purpose of this portion is to create open discussions to communicate your pain so that healing, empowerment, and purpose can be birthed. If we know the facts (our personal evaluation) then we know that we need to be rooted in the truth (Word of God).

1. How do you deal with pain?

   _____

   _____

_____

_____

_____

_____

_____

_____

_____

_____

2. What are some ways that you have helped others cope with pain?

_____

_____

_____

_____

_____

_____

_____

_____

_____

_____

3. Is there someone you need to forgive? (Let the process begin now)

_____

_____

_____

_____

_____

_____

_____

_____

_____

_____

4. Have you or do you have any
   addictions?

_____

_____

_____

_____

_____

_____

_____

_____

_____

_____

Please seek the necessary help- your LIFE depends on it!

5. Reflect- Have you embraced the purpose in your pain?

_____

_____

_____

_____

_____

_____

_____

_____

_____

_____

6. Have you ever dealt with heartbreak and how did you cope?

_____
_____
_____
_____
_____
_____
_____
_____
_____
_____

7. Having issues in your relationship/marriage? Have you reexamined yourself as well?

_____

_____

_____

_____

_____

_____

_____

_____

_____

_____

There are times when we point the finger instead of fixing our own wrong.

8. What are you doing to increase your prayer life? Prayer is conducive when you are experiencing pain.

_____

_____

_____

_____

_____

_____

_____

_____

_____

_____

9. Have you ever experienced suicidal thoughts? It is important to seek the necessary help

_____

_____

_____

_____

_____

_____

_____

_____

_____

_____

10. Discuss with someone or your prayer group, your experience of finding purpose in your pain.

Angie Taylor Reames

NOTES:

_____

_____

_____

_____

_____

_____

_____

_____

_____

_____

_____

_____

_____

I just want to personally encourage you that there is life after pain. I know that there are times when it seems like it is just too much- but let me encourage you to push. Just as in natural delivery, a woman must push in order to birth her baby. You must continue to push so that you can birth your purpose. It is in you; stay connected to God and trust in Him to get out of you what He gave you. You are a survivor and God has great things in store for you,

You are destined to be greater than that family curse. You are called to more than what the gossipers say about you. Your future has more success in it than your dreams. But you must trust God and also believe that you can do it. When you look around and no one else is there, please know that God is ALWAYS with you.

Angie Taylor Reames

I pray this prayer- Depression does not own you, Suicidal thoughts do not own you, Oppression must flee, Family curses must be broken, Broken hearts are healing. I rebuke any satanic attack on your life in the name of Jesus. Marriages are being mended and addiction will no longer be a weakness. The mind games of emotional abuse and the bruises of physical abuse have ended. I speak life over every person reading this and I pray that although life comes with pain- that we shall live and not die. I pray that our legacies will stand on a solid rock with our names on it, and we shall be free from bondage. Our life depends on our purpose and today we will operate in what God has called us to be. Thank you Jesus! Healing is already taking place and we say that it is done. Amen!

God Bless You.

There Is Purpose In Your Pain

Author

Angie Taylor Reames

Angie Taylor Reames

Angie Taylor Reames, author of Perfect Imperfection- I am who I am has written her second book in hopes that she can encourage someone to find their purpose. This book was written to encourage the reader that there is purpose in their pain. So often, we try to find suffering in pain and at times we dwell on the bad things until we are unable to see the good coming out of the situation. When pain is experienced we run from the cure because we are so afraid of the truth. Well, this author wants you to be encouraged in knowing that the pain is not what you should be focused on but the *purpose* in the pain. This interactive book is filled with inspiration, motivation, and the love of the Lord. Be inspired with information shared that will challenge you to operate in your purpose and coming in contact with who you really are.

Angie is married to the amazing Mr. Antowine Reames and together they have six wonderful children. She is an inspirational speaker, an advocate for youth, founder, and author. Angie aspires to inspire, encouraging others to be the best that they can be. She believes that there are occurrences when we must do a personal interview with ourselves so that we can operate at the best of our natural and spiritual ability. Angie loves people. She enjoys family time, laughter, helping people, and ministering to those that need to be loved, appreciated, and desire a sense of understanding. She is known for always having a smile on her face and she says, "You never know when Jesus is returning, so greet Him with a smile". When you see Mrs. Reames, you will definitely be greeted with a smile and the love of the Lord.